Landforms

Greg Roza

Rosen Classroom Books & Materials™
New York

A **landform** is any natural **feature** on Earth's **surface**.

A mountain is a rocky landform that rises above Earth's surface.

A **valley** is a landform between mountains or hills.

A desert is a dry landform that gets little rain.

Wind and water can change landforms.

People can change landforms too.

Glossary

feature An important part or quality of something.

landform One of the features that makes up Earth's surface.

surface The outermost layer of something.

valley An area of low ground between two hills, usually containing a river.